Teaching Language Arts
with the Internet

A companion Web site for this book is maintained at:

URL: http://twi.classroom.com/languagearts/k6

Acknowledgments

Senior Product Developers: Seija Surr, Joe Todaro
Writer: Kim Thoman
Production Manager: Kathleen Housley
Production Designer: Sam Gorgone
Art Buyer: Jane Leibowitz
Manufacturing: Benjamin Cintas

Due to the changing nature of the Internet, site addresses and their content may vary. Great care has been put into the selection of the very best Web sites for this series. But, no long term assurances can be made regarding their suitability for school use. Please visit the companion Web site for this product for updated addresses.

Classroom Connect
Corporate Offices
2221 Rosecrans Avenue, Suite 221
El Segundo, CA 90245

Classroom Connect
Product Development Offices
1241 East Hillsdale Boulevard
Foster City, CA 94404

URL: http://www.classroom.com
Email: connect@classroom.com
(800) 638-1639

All terms mentioned in this book that are known to be trademarks or service marks have been appropriately capitalized.

Printed in the United States of America.

1 2 3 4 5 6 7 8 9 10 - 02 01 00 99 98

ISBN: 1-58282-012-0

Product Code: TWI-1041

Teaching Language Arts
with the Internet

Internet Lesson Plans and Classroom Activities

classroom
CONNECT

2221 Rosecrans Ave., Suite 221
El Segundo, CA 90245
URL: http://www.classroom.com
Email: connect@classroom.com
(800) 638-1639

TABLE OF CONTENTS

INTRODUCTION

Welcome! We're happy that you are one of the growing number of classroom teachers who are excited about the incredible educational resources available on the Internet. We hope you will find many valuable nuggets in the lesson plans we have created to augment your Language Arts curriculum. Every lesson in this book integrates Internet resources into your classroom via online and offline activities.

This book is chock full of lesson plans that will enhance even the most innovative teacher's classroom. Your students will find it motivating to read online stories, poems, newspaper articles, game directions, jokes, and folk tales from around the world. They will also have a chance to use online resources such as dictionaries and lists of homophones. Students' offline activities include pre-writing organizational tasks, writing poetry, and writing a telephone dialog between two characters in a story. You'll be able to use these lesson plans and activity sheets "as is" or adapt them to suit your particular needs.

It's been said that the Internet is our present-day wild west. Here at Classroom Connect our authors and editors are enthusiastic about the inroads we're making toward taming this frontier for your classroom use.

We hope that you find as much enjoyment and value incorporating our lesson plans into your curriculum as we found in creating them for you. Every time we write a book, we learn more and more about the Web, its resources, and its ever-expanding network of connections—and we continue to be enthusiastic, even though we're still learning about the tip of the "Internet iceberg." This keeps us growing, thinking, changing, and reassessing—just like the perfect classroom!

We hope you will join us on this great adventure. Let us know what you think!

RHYMING FUN!

Overview

Children always have fun with words that rhyme. In this lesson they visit a Sesame Street Web site and look for pictures of things that rhyme with a given word. As a bonus, students can do the Web site's letter recognition activity.

Time Frame

One 45-minute session

Objectives

• Identify words that rhyme.
• Recognize letters of the alphabet.

Materials

• Computer with Internet access

Procedure

❶ Introduce the activity with a rhyming game. Tell students to think of animal names that rhyme with a word you say. Here are some words and the animal names that students might come up with.

big	pig
hat	cat, bat, rat
log	frog, hog
hair	bear, mare
knee	bee, flea

❷ Next, tell students to find things in the classroom that rhyme with a word you say. Here are some words and objects that students might see in the classroom that rhyme with each word.

fable	table
float	coat
dirt	shirt
more	door, floor
blue	shoe

❸ Have students go to the Sesame Street Activities Web site by typing the URL below into your browser or by clicking on the link on the Teaching Language Arts with the Internet Web page.

Sesame Street Activities
URL: http://www.sesamestreet.com/sesame/activities

❹ Explain to students that they will look for things in the pictures that rhyme with a word on their worksheet. They can show their answers by drawing a picture of the object.

❺ Point out that there are several hidden letters in each picture. If students can find all the letters, they will see a brief animation.

⚛ Extension

Invite students to return to the Web site investigate some of the other pictures. Have them draw a picture of an object they see. Let partners swap drawings with each other and try to think up words that rhyme with the objects they drew. It could be hard for the students to think up words for some of the pictures, so this might be a time to encourage students to have fun with nonsense words.

RHYMING FUN!

NAME:_____

DATE:_____

Go to the Sesame Street Web site at the URL below.

Sesame Street Activities
URL: http://sesamestreet.com/sesame/activities

Find an object in each picture that rhymes with the word. Draw the object in the box.

1. Click on *Big Bird Goes Camping*.

RENT

2. Click on *Telly's Circus Act*.

CAT

Find an object in each picture that rhymes with the word. Draw the object in the box.

3. Click on *Conductor Cookie on his Train.*

JOKE

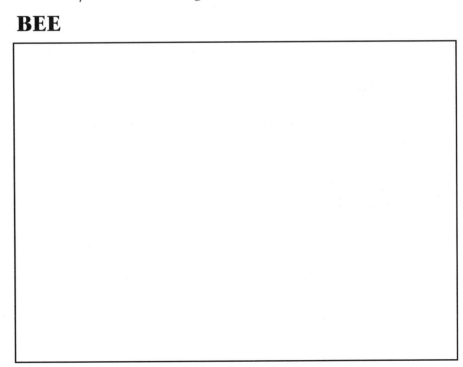

4. Click on *Betty Lou Goes Hiking.*

BEE

Beside, Below, Above, and More

Overview

In this lesson, students look at pictures on a Web site to find objects that show position words. Students will enjoy discovering that the pictures were drawn by children from other countries.

Time Frame

Two 45-minute sessions

Objectives

- Demonstrate position words.
- Read position words.
- Identify the position of objects.

Materials

- Computer with Internet access
- Crayons or colored pencils (optional)

Procedure

1 Write the following position words and phrases on the chalkboard.

beside	below
above	next to
on the right	on the left
in the middle	

As an introductory activity, tell students they will work in groups of three to plan how to demonstrate one of the positions or phrases. Explain that they are to demonstrate the word or phrase, in two different ways. Briefly discuss some of the ways that they might go about doing a demonstration. Suggestions that students might come up with include: drawing on the chalkboard, using objects in the room, using their own body positions, or leading the class in a demonstration.

2 Assign one of the words or phrases to each group and provide time for them to plan their demonstrations and do them for the class.

3 Invite students to go to the Animal Gallery at the URL below to find pictures of animals drawn by children. You can either type the URL into your browser or click on the link on the Teaching Language Arts with the Internet Web page.

Animal Gallery
URL: http://www.kids-space.org/gallery/_animals/_animals.html

Have students look for objects in the pictures that show position words. Their activity sheet tells them which pictures to click on and the position words. You may need to help students navigate around the site to find the required pictures.

Extensions

1 After completing the activity sheet, students might want to explore more about each picture. There is a small flag beside each picture. It's the flag of the country the artist is from. Clicking on it brings up a world map with all the flags plotted. To find some of these flags, good eyesight is essential—just the kind of searching children can get into. You might have students select a favorite picture, draw the flag of the country that the artist is from, and plot it on a classroom map.

2 Clicking on a blue bean next to a picture brings up a story about the picture. If students want to write their own stories about a picture, they can click on *write a story* at the top of the Animal Gallery's first page. Or, they can illustrate a story in the storybook section by clicking on *illustrate*.

3 Finally, you might want to lead students through the process of submitting a picture or story of their own. They can do this by clicking *Submit* at the top of the page.

BESIDE, BELOW, ABOVE, AND MORE

NAME: _____

DATE: _____

Go to the Animal Gallery at the URL below.

Animal Gallery
URL: http://www.kids-space.org/gallery/_animals/_animals.html

Find objects to show the words. Draw them.

1. Click on the picture by Serena.

ABOVE

BELOW

2. Go to Animal Gallery Room 10. Click on the picture by Mayu Itou.

BESIDE

BESIDE

3. Go to Animal Gallery Room 14. Click on the picture by Nadine Scott.

LEFT

MIDDLE

RIGHT

How Do Colors Make You Feel?

Overview

We all have our favorite and less preferred colors—often because we associate a particular color with a certain feeling. Poets and writers know the power of color association to enhance expression. In this lesson students visit a link of the Suessville Web site that lets them change the color of a gingerbread man to a color that they feel like today. Then they write how each of the colors makes them feel.

Time Frame

One 45-minute session

Objectives

• Use color association to enhance creative thinking.
• Use descriptive words to explain feelings.

Materials

• Computer with Internet access
• Crayons

 # Procedure

1 Ask students to name their favorite color and tell why it is their favorite. You might also want to ask whether anyone used to have a different favorite color and why they changed. Continue the discussion by asking what color is their least favorite and why.

2 Have students go to the Seussville Web site at the URL below. Click on *What Color are Your Days?* and follow the blue finger to read a story and do a short activity.

Seussville
URL: http://www.randomhouse.com/seussville/titles/days

3 Have students complete the activity sheet. As they change the color of the gingerbread man they should write how each of the colors makes them feel.

4 Wrap up the activity by printing out the gingerbread man and photocopying enough copies so that each student can color one with their favorite color. You might want to have students put their gingerbread men on the wall to create a pictograph showing how many in the class chose each different color as their favorite.

HOW DO COLORS MAKE YOU FEEL?

NAME:_____

DATE:_____

Go to the Seussville Web site at the URL below.

Seussville
URL: http://www.randomhouse.com/seussville/titles/days

Click *What Color are Your Days?* and follow the blue finger. Click on the color to change the gingerbread man. Write how each color makes you feel.

1. blue

_____

_____

_____

2. green

_____

_____

_____

3. pink

_____

_____

_____

4. purple

_____

_____

_____

5. orange

_____

_____

_____

6. black

_____

_____

_____

7. red

_____

_____

_____

8. gray

_____

_____

_____

9. yellow

_____

_____

_____

10. brown

_____

_____

_____

BEFORE AND AFTER ERNIE

Overview

In this lesson, the students examine a picture of Ernie watering his plant. Then they draw pictures to show what could have come before and what might come after.

Time Frame

One 45-minute session

Objectives

- Analyze visual information.
- Create mental images from pictures.
- Draw pictures to convey content.

Materials

- Computer with Internet access
- Wastebasket
- Crayons

Procedure

1 Introduce this activity by asking students to pretend to be movie directors. Explain that people who make movies have to be able to imagine things that come before and things that come after.

② Place a full wastebasket on a table top and tell the class that this is "now." Then explain that the movie director wants a scene that looks like it happened "before" or earlier in time. Ask students to suggest how to make the wastebasket show "before." They might suggest showing the wastebasket half full, an empty wastebasket, or a tiny bit of trash in the wastebasket.

③ Next explain that the movie director needs a scene that shows "later." Ask what the trash can could look like to show "later." Students might suggest a wastebasket piled even higher with trash, trash spilling over the top, or an empty wastebasket (after it has been emptied).

④ Have children go to the picture of Ernie at the URL below.

Sesame Street Activities
URL: http://www.sesamestreet.com/sesame/activities/hl/5/1a.htm

Have students draw pictures on their activity sheets to show what could have come before and what might come after the scene of Ernie watering his plants.

⑤ As an added bonus activity, tell students that the picture of Ernie has letters hidden in it. When all the letters are found, the computer offers a reward of a brief animation.

⑥ When students finish their drawings, you might want to print out the picture of Ernie watering his flowers and use it, and the students' drawings, to create a bulletin board showing *Before*, *Now*, and *After*.

BEFORE AND AFTER ERNIE

NAME:_____

DATE:_____

Go to the picture of Ernie at this Web site.

Sesame Street Activities
URL: http://www.sesamestreet.com/sesame/activities/hl/5/1a.htm

1. Draw a picture to show *Before*.

BEFORE AND AFTER ERNIE
. . . .

2. Draw a picture to show *After*.

SOUNDS THAT LETTERS SOUND LIKE

Overview

Before children are able to become proficient readers, they need experience recognizing letter sounds. In this lesson, students are given a letter and they draw the animal whose name begins with it.

Time Frame

One 45-minute session

Objectives

• Recognize the sounds of letters.
• Discriminate initial consonant sounds of words.

Materials

• Computer with Internet access
• Crayons

Procedure

1 You may want to introduce this lesson by saying the name of an object in the room and having students tell what letter it begins with. Next, alter the activity by pointing to an object in the classroom, without saying its name, and asking students to tell what letter it begins with. Finally, write a letter on the chalkboard and ask students to find an object in the room that begins with the letter.

2 Tell students they will do a similar activity on the computer. Have them go to the Animal Alphabet site at the URL below.

Animal Alphabet
URL: http://www.mrtc.org/~twright/animals/english/alphquiz.htm

3 Students can click on a letter of the alphabet and see pictures of animals. They should decide which animal's name begins with the letter and show their answer by drawing a picture of the animal. Their activity sheet tells them which letters to click on.

4 Students can check to see if their choices are correct by clicking on the picture of the animal. The computer will let them know if they made the correct choice. To return to the alphabet page, students can use the Back button on their browser.

SOUNDS THAT LETTERS SOUND LIKE

NAME:_____

DATE:_____

Go to this Animal Alphabet Web site.

Animal Alphabet
URL: http://www.mrtc.org/~twright/animals/english/alphquiz.htm

Draw a picture of the animal whose name begins with each letter.

1. Click on *L*.

L

2. Click on *B*.

B

3. Click on *Q*.

```
Q
```

4. Click on *R*.

```
R
```

Ask the Cat!

Overview

For years, Dr. Seuss books have charmed children and parents alike. We all have our favorite characters or can quote a line from *The Cat in the Hat* or *Green Eggs and Ham*. In this activity, students visit the Dr. Seuss Web site and read some fun questions to ask the Cat. Then they write up their own questions and come up with make-believe answers for each other's questions.

Time Frame

Two 45-minute sessions

Objectives

- Write complete sentences.
- Use conventions of capitalization.
- Use question marks after interrogative sentences.

Materials

- Computer with Internet access
- Email account (optional)
- Dr. Seuss books (optional)

Procedure

1 If possible, introduce this lesson by reading *The Cat in the Hat* to the class—even if students have heard it before they will love to hear it one more time.

❷ Tell students they will visit a Web site called *Ask the Cat!* At the site they will read some examples of fun questions to ask the Cat and then they will write some of their own questions for the Cat. Before students go to the computer, however, review the conventions for writing questions: use of a complete sentence, capitalizing the first letter of the first word, and ending with a question mark.

❸ Have students go to the Ask the Cat! Web page at the URL below.

Ask the Cat!
URL: http://www.randomhouse.com/seussville/askthecat

❹ After students read the questions on the Web page, have them write their own questions on their activity sheets. If possible, encourage students to scan some Dr. Seuss books to help them think up good questions to ask the Cat. Then explain that partners will switch papers and write the Cat's answers for each other's questions.

If students have access to an email account, they can click on the questions on the Web page and request a reply from the Webmaster Cat!

ASK THE CAT!

NAME:_____

DATE:_____

Go to the Ask the Cat! Web page.

Ask the Cat!
URL: http://www.randomhouse.com/seussville/askthecat

Read some questions for the cat. Then make up some of your own questions to ask the cat.

Question 1

_____

_____

Cat's Answer

_____

_____

Question 2

_____

_____

Cat's Answer

_____

_____

Question 3

_____

_____

Cat's Answer

_____

_____

Question 4

_____

_____

Cat's Answer

_____

_____

Question 5

_____

_____

Cat's Answer

_____

_____

ASK THE CAT!

CHECKING OUT AN ONLINE DICTIONARY

Overview

In this lesson, students use an online picture dictionary to look up the definitions of some unfamiliar words.

Time Frame

One 45-minute session

Objectives

- Locate words in an online dictionary.
- Write the definitions of unfamiliar words.

Materials

- Computer with Internet access

Procedure

1 Students can do this straightforward dictionary activity with little or no introduction. Have students go to the Little Explorers Picture Dictionary at the URL below.

Little Explorers Picture Dictionary
URL: http://www.LittleExplorers.com/Dictionarytitlepage.html

Students should click on *browse through the dictionary* to get started.

TEACHING LANGUAGE ARTS WITH THE INTERNET

❷ Have students look up each word on the activity sheets and write the definitions on their activity sheets.

Extension

As a follow-up activity, you can have students look up the words in a print dictionary and compare the definitions with the ones they found online.

CHECKING OUT AN ONLINE DICTIONARY

NAME:_____

DATE:_____

Go to the dictionary at this Web site.

Little Explorers Picture Dictionary
URL: http://www.LittleExplorers.com/Dictionarytitlepage.html

Find these words in the dictionary. Write their definitions.

1. vat

_____

_____

_____

2. arch

_____

_____

_____

3. kin

_____

_____

_____

4. ellipse

_____

_____

_____

5. Venus flytrap

_____

_____

_____

6. meerkat

_____

_____

_____

7. quetzal

_____

_____

_____

8. kazoo

_____

_____

_____

SOME SYNONYMS AND ANTONYMS

Overview

Students explore a link on the Mr. Roger's Neighborhood Web site to find a picture of King Friday XIII who rules the Neighborhood of Make-Believe. On their activity sheets, they read about the King and replace some words with synonyms and others with antonyms (opposites). Then, if a printer is available, students can download the line drawing of the King and color him to match their sentences.

Time Frame

One 45-minute session

Objectives

- Give examples of synonyms.
- Give examples of antonyms (opposites).
- Follow written directions.

Materials

- Computer with Internet access
- Crayons

Procedure

1 To introduce the activity, write the sentence below on the chalkboard, underlining the word *love*.

Kids <u>love</u> to do homework.

Explain to students that you aren't so sure this is true, so you'd like to change to word *love* to a word that means its opposite. Ask the students for word ideas and list them on the board. Some words that the students might suggest include *hate* or *dislike*.

Write the word *antonyms* on the chalkboard and explain that it means words that have the opposite meanings from each other.

2 Write another sentence on the chalkboard, underlining the word *love* again as shown below.

Kids <u>love</u> to eat candy.

This time explain that you think this might be true and ask the students to come up with some words that can replace the word *love* but not change the meaning of the sentence. Students may suggest the words such as *like* or *enjoy*. Again, write these words and the word *synonyms* on the chalkboard. Explain that synonyms are words that have the same meaning.

3 Have students go to the *Coloring King Friday* link on the Mr. Roger's Neighborhood Web site at the URL below to find a drawing of King Friday.

Mr. Roger's Neighborhood
URL: http://www.pbs.org/rogers/color3.html

4 Have students read sentences about the King on their activity sheets and then write synonyms and antonyms for some of the words.

5 When students are finished writing, you might want to print out the picture of King Friday and make photocopies so that students can color him to match the sentences they have written.

SOME SYNONYMS AND ANTONYMS

NAME:_____

DATE:_____

Go to the King Friday Web page.

Mr. Rogers' Neighborhood
URL: http://www.pbs.org/rogers/color3.html

Write each sentence over, using synonyms for the underlined words.

1. King Friday's crown has <u>lots of</u> colors in it.

_____

_____

_____

2. He has a <u>sparkle</u> in his eye.

_____

_____

_____

3. The King's gown is a <u>pretty</u> color.

_____

_____

_____

Write each sentence over, using antonyms for the underlined words.

4. King Friday's cape is <u>light</u> blue.

_____

_____

_____

5. The King and Queen live in a <u>huge</u> castle.

_____

_____

_____

6. The King is often <u>sad</u>.

_____

_____

_____

WHAT'S THE TITLE?

Overview

Even at a young age, children can appreciate and enjoy looking at the masterpieces of the art world. In this lesson, students visit an educational site that has compiled a variety of world-famous paintings. They examine some paintings and then use their observations to come up with new titles. Of course, students may also enjoy browsing through all the paintings and selecting their favorite!

Time Frame

One 45-minute session

Objectives

- Interpret meaning from visual information.
- Create and write titles for artwork.
- Verbalize personal opinions.

Materials

- Computer with Internet access
- Several pictures of paintings from art books, magazines, or posters, including some that show people in action (optional)

# Procedure

1 Ask students to tell about any pictures they have hanging in their family homes, such as paintings, drawings, prints, photographs, or posters. Ask if they know the title of the works. Most students probably will not know titles, so you can invite them to find out the titles and bring this information back to share with the class.

2 You may want to continue by showing some pictures of paintings from books or magazines. Have students describe what they see in the pictures and then have them make up titles that fit their observations.

3 Have students go to the Eyes on Art Web site at the URL below to find masterpieces of people, places, and things. Have them scroll down to find the small versions of the paintings. They can click on these to see larger versions.

Eyes on Art
URL: http://www.kn.pacbell.com/wired/art/choose.html

4 Ask students to look closely at the details in a painting and make up a new title that fits the picture. Their activity sheet tells them which paintings to choose.

5 When students have finished writing new titles, have a class discussion comparing students' choices of new titles.

Activity
Sheet
9

WHAT'S THE TITLE?

NAME:_____

DATE:_____

Go to the Eyes on Art Web site.

Eyes on Art
URL: http://www.kn.pacbell.com/wired/art/choose.html

Scroll down to find the small paintings. Click on each to make it bigger.
Write a new title.

1. Click on *Las Meninas*. (Can you find the mirror?)

New Title:

_____

_____

2. Click on *Cliff Dwellers*.

New Title:

_____

_____

3. Click on *People in the Sun*.

New Title:

_____

_____

4. Click on *No Swimming*. (Why are the boys running?)

New Title:

_____

_____

5. Click on *A Sunday Afternoon at the Isle of the Grande Jatte*. (Can you find the monkey?)

New Title:

_____

_____

6. Click on *Point of Tranquility*.

New Title:

_____

_____

TEDDY BEAR RHYMES

Overview

Students read the *Teddy Bear, Teddy Bear* nursery rhyme on The Mother Goose Web site. They identify the words that rhyme and then use other rhyming words to make up new verses.

Time Frame

One 45-minute session

Objectives

• Identify words that rhyme.
• Write in poem format.
• Read poetry aloud.

Materials

• Computer with Internet access

 # Procedure

1 For younger students, introduce the lesson by asking them to stand and act out the poem as you read the following nursery rhyme.

> Teddy bear, Teddy bear
> Touch the ground.
> Teddy bear, Teddy bear
> Turn around.
> Teddy bear, Teddy bear
> Show your shoe.
> Teddy bear, Teddy bear
> That will do.
> Teddy bear, Teddy bear
> Run upstairs.
> Teddy bear, Teddy bear
> Say your prayers.
> Teddy bear, Teddy bear
> Blow out the light.
> Teddy bear, Teddy bear
> Say good night.

Let students do it several times. By the second or third time, see if students can remember the second line of each rhyme.

2 Have students go to The Mother Goose site at the URL below to read the Teddy Bear nursery rhyme.

Mother Goose
URL: http://pubweb.acns.nwu.edu/~pfa/dreamhouse/nursery/rhymes/
teddy.html

3 On their activity sheets, have students write the words that rhyme in the poem and then make up some new verses.

4 Combine all the new Teddy bear verses and have different volunteers read them for the class.

TEDDY BEAR RHYMES

NAME:_____

DATE:_____

Go to The Mother Goose Web site.

Mother Goose
URL: http://pubweb.acns.nwu.edu/~pfa/dreadhouse/nursery/rhymes/
teddy.html

Write the word that rhymes with each.

1. ground

_____

_____

2. shoe

_____

_____

3. upstairs

_____

_____

4. light

_____

_____

Write a sentence the ends with the word. Then write the next line so it rhymes!

Teddy bear, Teddy bear

_____nose.

Teddy bear, Teddy bear

_____

Teddy bear, Teddy bear

_____knees.

Teddy bear, Teddy bear

_____

Teddy bear, Teddy bear

_____feet.

Teddy bear, Teddy bear

_____

LOOKING FOR CONTRACTIONS

Overview

In this activity, students review contractions and then visit a Web site of rhymes and nonsense. They read some of the rhymes and write down the contractions that they find. To wrap up the activity, students read a rhyme aloud—with and without the contractions—and discuss how the contractions help the flow of the rhyme.

Time Frame

One 45-minute session

Objectives

• Identify contractions.
• Read aloud.
• Use critical listening.

Materials

• Computer with Internet access

 # Procedure

1 Write several contractions on the chalkboard, such as the ones below. Have students tell the two words that each contraction stands for. Explain that the apostrophe in the contraction is the substitute for the letters that are left out.

she'll	she will
shouldn't	should not
you're	you are
he's	he is
we're	we are
she'd	she would

2 Next write several phrases showing the possessive. Explain that the apostrophe is used to show that the object is owned. Discuss with students how contractions and possessives can look alike, but have very different meanings.

Tom's hat
cat's tail
dog's paw
girl's jacket

3 Have students go to the Rhymes and Nonsense page at the URL below. You can either type the URL into your browser or click on the link on the Teaching Language Arts with the Internet Web page.

Rhymes and Nonsense
URL: http://www.thekids.com/kids/stories/rhymes

Have students click on each title and read the rhyme. On the activity sheets, they should write the contractions or possessives that they find.

4 When students finish their activity sheets, print out and photocopy *Polly, Put the Kettle On*. Have students practice reading it aloud, with the contractions, and then with the two words that make up the contraction. Invite the class to decide if the contraction makes it easier to read or changes the flow of the rhyme.

LOOKING FOR CONTRACTIONS

NAME:_____

DATE:_____

Go to the Rhymes and Nonsense page at this URL.

Rhymes and Nonsense
URL: http://www.thekids.com/kids/stories/rhymes

Write the contractions or possessives you find. Also write the words that the contractions stand for. Circle the word if it's a possessive. Write *none* if you don't find any.

1. Click on *A Thing of Beauty Is a Joy Forever*.

_____

_____

_____

_____

_____

2. Click on *Polly, Put the Kettle On*.

_____

_____

_____

_____

_____

3. Click on *Baa Baa Black Sheep*.

_____

_____

_____

4. Click on *Old King Cole*.

_____

_____

_____

5. Click on *The North Wind Doth Blow*.

_____

_____

_____

6. Click on *I Had a Little Pony*.

_____

_____

_____

A FISH FABLE

Overview

In this lesson, students read *The Three Fish* from the Fables of Bidpai. They use a Venn diagram to answer questions about the fable and then discuss the meaning of the story.

Time Frame

Two 45-minute sessions

Objectives

• Recall details from a story.
• Use a Venn diagram to record answers to questions.
• Understand the point of a fable.

Materials

• Computer with Internet access

 # Procedure

1 Tell students that they will read a fable titled *The Three Fish*, from an ancient collection of stories from India, called the Fables of Bidpai. Explain that some of the Fables of Bidpai were thought to have been written down for the first time more than two thousand years ago; before that they were passed along orally. You might mention that little is known of the person called Bidpai, and some don't even think he existed. Click on *Fables of Bidpai*, on the first page of the online story for more detailed information.

The Three Fish
URL: http://www.thekids.com/kids/stories/fables/fish/fish.html

2 Discuss with students the difference between a fable and other kinds of stories. Tell students that fables are usually stories that are intended to give moral instruction. If students are familiar with an Aesop fable, such as *The Hare and the Tortoise* or *The Ant and the Grasshopper*, you might briefly let them tell the story and its moral.

3 Have students go to The Three Fish page at the URL above and read the story. Or, print out the three-page story ahead of time and make copies for students to read. To visit the site, you can either type the URL into your browser or click on the link on the Teaching Language Arts with the Internet Web page.

4 After reading the story, have students answer the questions on their activity sheets by making a mark in the appropriate area of each Venn diagram. If needed, review how this type of graphic organizer works. For example, if an answer to a question is "Wise Fish and Clever Fish," students should mark the intersection of those two circles.

5 Conclude the activity with a discussion about what the story tells us. Encourage students to share ideas about what the story says about human nature.

A Fish Fable

NAME:_____

DATE:_____

Go to The Three Fish Web page.

> **The Three Fish**
> URL: http://www.thekids.com/kids/stories/fables/fish/fish.html

Answer each question by marking the diagram.

1. Which fish pretended to be dead?

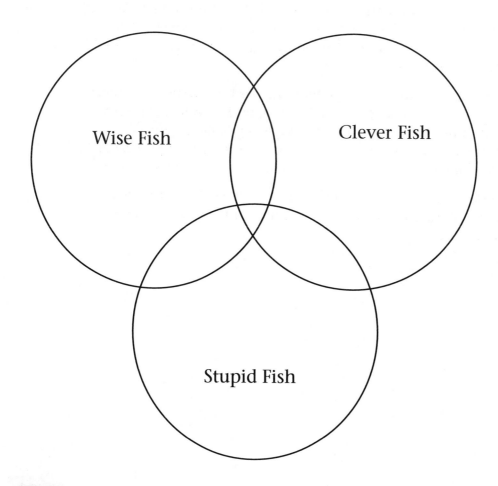

2. Which fish shared the pool for many years?

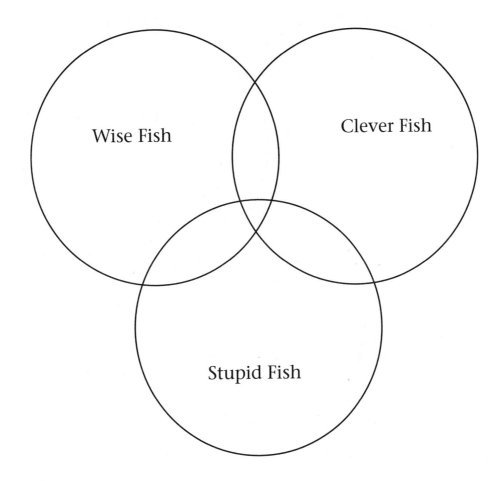

3. Which fish got away from the fishermen?

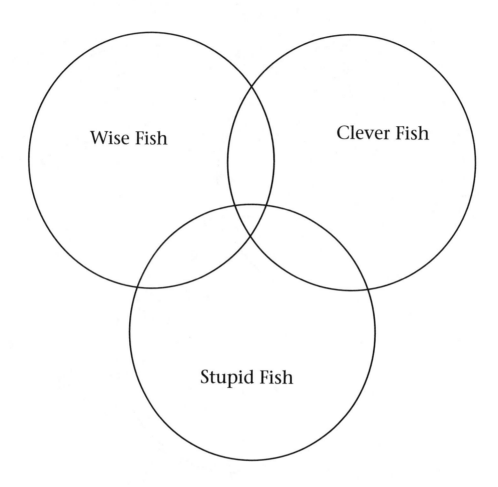

Wise Fish

Clever Fish

Stupid Fish

4. Which fish relied on Clever Fish?

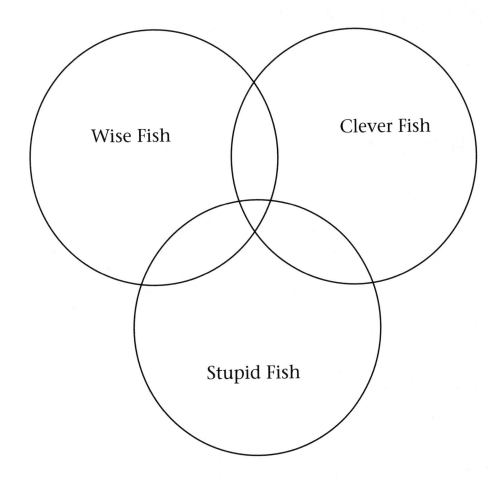

CROSSWORD PUZZLES

Overview

In this lesson, students come up with the words and clues for a crossword puzzle and then—*voila!*—the computer creates it. This is a great activity for students to do online, because the computer does a lot of the work! But plenty of student thinking, planning, and reworking is required to create these crossword puzzles. As all of us know with computers, what you get is only as good as what you put in. The students' task is not only to come up with interesting clues for their words, but to figure out how to make sure the computer uses every single one of them.

Time Frame

Two 45-minute sessions

Objectives

- Use word meanings to write puzzle clues.
- Evaluate peers' work to improve or clarify meaning.
- Revise work to incorporate suggestions from peers.

Materials

- Computer with Internet access
- Sample crossword puzzle from a newspaper (optional)

 # Procedure

1 You might want to begin by showing students the crossword puzzle in a local newspaper. Discuss with students how a crossword puzzle works. Write the words *ten* and *boy* on the chalkboard and ask if a crossword puzzle could be made out of just these two words. Make sure students understand that a puzzle could not be made from just these two words because they don't contain any of the same letters—there would be no way to connect them. Then write the words *girl* and *dog* on the chalkboard and ask if a puzzle could be made using just these two words. This time, be sure the students understand that a puzzle is possible because the two words contain the letter *g*. Show how *dog* could be written vertically to connect the *g* with the word *girl*.

2 Point out that sometimes crossword puzzles have a theme. Tell students they are going to create a crossword puzzle online, and ask students what they might use as a theme or topic. Some ideas students might include: school, your city, games, food, sports, or animals.

3 Discuss the clues for words. Point out that clues can be given in many different ways—and this is where students can use their creativity. Have the class brainstorm lots of different clues that could be given for the word *moon*. If necessary, suggest some of the following to get ideas flowing.

- The cow jumped over it.
- Sun and _____.
- Some say it's made of green cheese.
- The man in the _____.

4 Pair students and have them go to the Criss Cross Setup Form at the URL below.

Puzzlemaker
URL: http://www.puzzlemaker.com/CrissCrossSetupForm.asp

5 Be sure students leave the default settings for the size of the puzzle and the size of the puzzle cells. Have pairs decide on a theme or topic and use it to title their puzzle. Then they can tab down to enter the words and clues.

6 As pairs decide on words and clues, have one partner write them on the Planning Section of the activity sheet while the other types them into the computer. Explain that the computer makes the puzzle and prints the clues, and will automatically eliminate words it can't use. On the same page that the puzzle is created, the computer tells how many of the words were used (in small type underneath the clues). Students will need to refer to their notes in their Planning Section to figure out what words to eliminate on the setup form. Their goal is to have every word used in the puzzle. When students have completed all the changes needed for their puzzle, have them make an Answer Key on the activity sheet. (The computer doesn't print out an answer sheet.)

7 When students finish their puzzles have them exchange them with other pairs. They can work the puzzles and give feedback on how easy or hard the clues were to figure out. Have students revise their puzzles accordingly.

Activity
Sheet
13

CROSSWORD PUZZLES

NAME: _____

DATE: _____

Go to the Criss Cross Setup Form at the URL below.

Puzzlemaker
URL: http://www.puzzlemaker.com/CrissCrossSetupForm.asp

Your task: Make a puzzle and be sure that all of your words are used in the puzzle.

Planning Section

Answer Key

LIZARDS FOR LUNCH

Overview

In this lesson students read an online story about a boy named Andy who brings home different kinds of animals from the pet store. In his quest for the most exciting pet, each animal causes some kind of problem. After reading this story, students are asked to pretend they are the author and lengthen the story.

Time Frame

Two 45-minute sessions

Objectives

- Apply reading skills.
- Create ideas for fiction writing.

Materials

- Computer with Internet access

Procedure

1 Introduce the lesson by asking the students to tell about the pets they own and what kinds of mischief their pets have gotten into. Did their dog chew up things when it was a puppy? Did their dog bark at cars or bite the mailman, or did their cat get into fights with other cats in the neighborhood?

❷ Tell students they will read a story called *Lizards for Lunch* about a boy named Andy who is looking for an exciting pet. In the story, Andy keeps bringing different animals home from the pet store—Waldo the elephant, LooLaBell the Lizard, and others—only to find that they cause all sorts of problems for him.

❸ Have students go to Children's Stories at the URL below and click on *Lizards for Lunch* to read the story online. Or, you can print out the four-page story ahead of time and make hard copies for students to read.

Children's Stories
URL: http://www.itsnet.com/~outward/childstory.html

❹ After students have read the story tell them to pretend that they are the author. The publisher says that the story is too short! They need to think up some more animals for Andy to bring home from the pet store and try out. And they have to think of what problems those animals gave Andy to make him take them back to the pet store.

❺ When students have completed their activity sheets, give them time to share some of their best ideas with the class. You may also want to have students take the ideas in their tables and write them up as stories.

LIZARDS FOR LUNCH

NAME:_____

DATE:_____

Go to the Children's Stories at the URL below.

Children's Stories
URL: http://www.itsnet.com/~outward/childstory.html

Click on *Lizards For Lunch* and read the story.

Think of some new animals for Andy to bring home from the pet store.
Write about why Andy takes it back to the pet store.

Kind of Animal	Animal's Name	Why Does Andy Take it Back to the Pet Store?

Kind of Animal	Animal's Name	Why Does Andy Take it Back to the Pet Store?

ADDING TO A STORY

Overview

Blue Bear is a delightful online story complete with colorful illustrations. Five pages of this fifteen page story, however, are full-spread illustrations without text—a perfect opportunity for students to add writing to accompany these illustrations and enhance the story.

Time Frame

Two 45-minute sessions

Objectives

• Write for a specific audience.
• Evaluate each other students' writing.

Materials

• Computer with Internet access

Procedure

1 Have students go to the Blue Bear page at the URL below to find the online story. Explain that *Blue Bear* is an online picture book with writing and pictures on some pages and just pictures on other pages.

Blue Bear
URL: http://www.dreambox.com/storybox/bluebear/bookone/cover.htm

2 After students read the story, explain that their job is to enhance the story by making up some writing for the pages that don't have any. Remind them that they must make their writing fit smoothly between the pages that already have writing.

3 When students finish, have them meet in small critique groups around the computer to read the story aloud—adding their parts when the full spreads come up. Alternatively, you could print out the story and have groups meet offline. Encourage students to comment on how well the additions fit the flow and enhance the story.

ADDING TO A STORY

NAME:_____

DATE:_____

Go to the Blue Bear Web page at the URL below.

Blue Bear
URL: http://www.dreambox.com/storybox/bluebear/bookone/cover.htm

Read the story and look at the pictures. Make up some writing for the five pages that do not have any words.

1.

2.

3.

4.

5.

CHORAL READINGS

Overview

Both you and your students will get some laughs at Kenn Nesbitt's Poetry for Kids Web site. First, have students read through the poems and rate how well they like them. Then, working with a partner, they can choose a poem, prepare a choral reading, and share it with the rest of the class.

Time Frame

Two 45-minute sessions

Objectives

• Apply reading skills.
• Prepare, practice, and perform a choral reading.

Materials

• Computer with Internet access

Procedure

1 To introduce the lesson, you may want to invite a student or a fellow faculty member to prepare with you, ahead of class, a choral reading of Kenn Nesbitt's poem *Sore Throat*, found at the Web site below.

Poetry for Kids
URL: http://www.poetry4kids.com/poems.html

Take turns reading alternate lines and read some lines in unison. Alternatively, make a copy of the poem and, in class, enlist a volunteer to read the poem with you. Invite the class to listen while you and the student practice it several times until you can do it smoothly. Introducing the activity this way may help demonstrate the value of ample rehearsal time.

2 Have pairs visit the Poetry For Kids Web site to find lots of poems by Kenn Nesbitt. Have pairs read them out loud to each other and rate them on their activity sheets. (This site is updated occasionally. If students can't find the poems on their activity sheets, have them replace these poems with new poems of their choice.)

3 Have pairs choose one poem and prepare a choral reading with their partner. Have students print out their poem and work with their partner to determine who says which lines and which lines are said together. Encourage them to try out several variations.

4 Let students do a rehearsal reading for the class. Then, when their readings are polished, arrange to have students perform for another class.

Extension

Assign a small team of students to compile the activity sheet surveys. They can make a graph showing the class's ratings of the poems.

CHORAL READINGS

NAME:_____

DATE:_____

With a partner, go to the Poetry For Kids Web site at the URL below to find lots of funny poems.

Poetry for Kids
URL: http://www.poetry4kids.com/poems.html

Circle a number to rate each poem.

> Ratings
> 10 means a great poem!
> 1 means it's the worst.

1. *Ancient*

    1   2   3   4   5   6   7   8   9   10

2. *Don't Bring Camels in the Classroom*

    1   2   3   4   5   6   7   8   9   10

3. *Fearless Frederick*

    1   2   3   4   5   6   7   8   9   10

4. *How Did You Get So Mean?*

    1   2   3   4   5   6   7   8   9   10

5. *My Father Looks Like Frankenstein*

    1   2   3   4   5   6   7   8   9   10

6. *One Lion*

    1   2   3   4   5   6   7   8   9   10

7. *Springy Sidewalk*

    1   2   3   4   5   6   7   8   9   10

8. *My Feet*

    1   2   3   4   5   6   7   8   9   10

9. *A Pig Is In My Wig*

    1   2   3   4   5   6   7   8   9   10

10. *My Dad's a Secret Agent*

    1   2   3   4   5   6   7   8   9   10

KID'S POEMS

Overview

At this Environmental Defense Fund Web site for kids, students read poetry inspired by our wondrous earth and its inhabitants. Students categorize the online poems as either a rhyming poem or free verse. Then they write their own poem, using either style, and illustrate it.

Time Frame

Two 45-minute sessions

Objectives

- Apply reading skills and strategies.
- Categorize different kinds of poems.
- Write an original poem.

Materials

- Computer with Internet access

Procedure

1 Write the terms *rhyming poem* and *free verse* on the chalkboard. Tell students you are going to read two poems and you want them to tell which kind of poem they think each is. Read the poems on page 69.

It's a Hard Life

All I do is schoolwork
While my dog just plays all day.
Then I do my homework
While my cat sleeps his life away.

My parents say, "Too bad,"
An "A" I'd better get.
I say, "It's a shame
I'm a person not a pet."

Sunshine

A ray stretches around my arm,
The warmth wraps like a rag.
The edges of the light flicker on my skin,
Making me wonder at the sun's long reach.

2 Be sure students recognize that *It's a Hard Life* is a rhyming poem and *Sunshine* is free verse. Have them tell which words in the rhyming poem rhyme. Then ask students to tell some of the differences between the two styles of poems. Students might suggest that a free verse poem seems more like complete sentences, free verse doesn't have any rhyming words, or free verse sounds more like natural talking.

3 Invite students to go to the Earth to Kids Web site at the URL below to read some children's poems about the environment. Solicit some comments about what they think the poems at an environmental Web site might be about. Students might mention the earth, animals, flowers, ocean, or rain.

Earth to Kids
URL: http://www.edf.org/Earth2Kids

4 Have students click on *Kid's Poems* and then click on a poem title. After reading each poem, they can either go forward to read the next poem or go back to select a title by clicking on *Earth to Kids* at the bottom of the page.

5 Have students write their own poem about the environment using either poetry style.

Extensions

1 Have students illustrate their poems and then submit them to the Web site by clicking on *Submit YOUR poem to Earth to Kids*.

2 Assign a literary journal editing team to pull together all the poems that students wrote. Emphasize the importance of making good decisions about the order of the poems in a journal. What might make a good first piece? What might be a good one to end with? How can the order of the poems keep the reader interested?

KID'S POEMS

NAME: _____

DATE: _____

Go to the Earth to Kids Web site at the URL below to find poems about the environment.

Earth to Kids
URL: http://www.edf.org/Earth2Kids

1. Click on *Kids' Poems*. Click on a poem's title to read it. List some titles to tell whether they are rhyming poems or free verse poems.

Rhyming Poems   Free Verse Poems

2. Write your own poem about the environment.

LETTERS TO THE EDITOR

 ## Overview

Students read the front page article of the Little Planet Times, an online newspaper. They do several pre-writing tasks and then write a final draft of a letter to the editor, expressing their point of view on the issue raised in the article.

 ## Time Frame

Three or four 45-minute sessions

 ## Objectives

- Use pre-writing strategies: taking notes, brainstorming, etc.
- Write with the purpose of explaining a point of view.
- Write drafts and revise work.
- Edit and evaluate other's work.

 ## Materials

- Computer with Internet access
- The editorial page from a local newspaper. Identify a short letter to the editor about a topic that might interest students.

 ## Procedure

1 Show students the editorial page of the local newspaper that you brought to class. Read one of the letters to the editor aloud, choosing one that is about a topic that might interest students.

2 Discuss with students how a letter to the editor in a newspaper is different from a letter they might write to a friend. Steer the conversation to help students understand that a letter to the editor must present a specific point of view. These letters are opinion pieces and the authors are trying to convince the reader to agree with their position on a subject.

3 Have students visit an online newspaper at the URL below. Without an introduction—the topic can be a fun surprise for students—have them read the front page article.

Little Planet Times
URL: http://littleplanettimes.com

4 After reading the article, the student's first pre-writing task is to jot down their first thoughts on the issue presented in the article.

5 After coming up with some of their own ideas, then have students click on *Letters* and read what others have said on the issue. Encourage students to jot down more notes when they read some good solutions or come across words or phases that help support their own opinions.

6 Gather the class together and explain that students' next job is to write a first draft of their letter to the editor. Lead a discussion on how to be effective when trying to convince someone to agree with your point of view.

7 After students write their first draft, pair them to read each other's letters and write suggestions for improvement. Remind partners to look for spelling and grammar errors as well as to consider whether the letter is convincing.

8 Finally, have students write the final draft of their letter to the editor. When finished, you might have students submit their letters to the Little Planet Times.

LETTERS TO THE EDITOR

NAME: _____

DATE: _____

Go to the Little Planet Times Web site at the URL below and read the front page article.

Little Planet Times
URL: http://littleplanettimes.com

What do you think should be done about the issue described on the front page?

_____

_____

_____

_____

_____

_____

What are some other possible solutions?

_____

_____

_____

_____

_____

_____

_____

First Draft of a Letter to the Editor

Partner's Comments on the Draft

_____

_____

_____

_____

_____

_____

_____

_____

_____

_____

_____

_____

_____

_____

_____

_____

Dear Editor of the Little Planet Times,

Sincerely,

KOKOTO

Overview

Kokoto is a game of concentration that students play online. As they discover the animals hidden under the rocks they read about each animal and decode vocabulary words using context clues. Then they confirm the words meanings by looking them up in a dictionary.

Time Frame

One 45-minute session

Objectives

- Derive vocabulary definitions from context.
- Use a dictionary to confirm word definitions.

Materials

- Computer with Internet access
- Dictionary (optional)
- Netscape Navigator 3.0 or Internet Explorer 3.0 (or higher) can be used to play the game. You also need the MacroMedia Shockwave plug-in. If you don't have it already, a popup message will come up to direct you to the Shockwave Download Center.

Procedure

1 This straightforward activity needs little introduction. Invite students to go to the Kokoto Web page at the URL below to play a game of concentration. Let students play the game several times without involving the activity sheets.

Kokoto
URL: http://www.edf.org/Earth2Kids/kokoto

2 After a bit of game playing, give students the activity sheets and have them play once more. This time, tell them to read about the animal when they make a match. Have students guess the definition of each of the vocabulary words and write it on their activity sheets.

3 After students finish guessing the definitions of the vocabulary words, have them use either an online or offline dictionary to look up the actual meaning of each word and write it on their activity sheets. Students can go to the URL below to find an online dictionary.

Online Dictionary
URL: http://www.m-w.com/dictionary.htm

KOKOTO

NAME:_____

DATE:_____

Go to the Kokoto Web site at the URL below to play a game of concentration.

Kokoto
URL: http://www.edf.org/Earth2Kids/kokoto

Read about each animal. Find the vocabulary word. Write what you think it means.

1. African Cheetah

   Word: marauding

   Guess the meaning _____

   Dictionary definition _____

2. Giant Tortoise

   Word: selective

   Guess the meaning _____

   Dictionary definition _____

3. Mountain Gorilla

   Word: poaching

   Guess the meaning _____

   Dictionary definition _____

....

4. Whooping Crane

Word: captive

Guess the meaning _____

Dictionary definition _____

5. Bald Eagle

Word: rebound

Guess the meaning _____

Dictionary definition _____

6. Black-Footed Ferret

Word: prey

Guess the meaning _____

Dictionary definition _____

7. Gray Wolf

Word: decades

Guess the meaning _____

Dictionary definition _____

8. Humpback Whale

Word: complex

Guess the meaning _____

Dictionary definition _____

9. West Indian Manatee

Word: placid

Guess the meaning _____

Dictionary definition _____

FOLK AND FAIRY TALES FROM AROUND THE WORLD

 ## Overview

Students visit a Web site that provides a selection of folk and fairy tales from around the world. After reading one, they identify the main characters and write the sequence of events that take place in the story. Students can use these activity sheet pages as cue cards while they retell the story to the class.

 ## Time Frame

Two 45-minutes sessions

 ## Objectives

• Identify main characters of a folk or fairy tale.
• Prepare a sequence of events.
• Retell stories.

 ## Materials

• Computer with Internet access

 ## Procedure

1 Ask your students to name their favorite fairy tale or folk tale. As students respond, have them name the main characters and give a brief summary of the order of events that take place in the story. You might also have students tell why the tale is their favorite.

❷ Tell students they will visit a Web site that has folk and fairy tales from other countries. The Web site lets students select tales from the locations or cultures listed below. Ask if any students' families have visited these places or are from these places.

Africa	Japan
Central Asia	Middle East
Central Europe	Native America
China	Russia
England	Scandinavia
India	Scotland
Ireland	Siberia

❸ Have students go to the Folk and Fairy Tales from Around the World Web site at the URL below. Have students click on a country and then choose a story to read.

Folk and Fairy Tales from Around the World
URL: http://darsie.ucdavis.edu/tales

❹ Ask students to complete the activity sheet to identify the main character and sequence the events that occurred in the story.

❺ Invite students to retell their story to the whole class or to a small group. Students can use their activity sheet pages as cue cards to help remember the main points.

❻ Round out the activity with a class discussion about the similarities and differences among the stories. Lead the conversation to help students understand that folk and fairy tales generally have a moral or are intended to instruct in some way.

Extensions

❶ As a geography exercise, have students use a map or globe to find the country that their story came from. Students can write the name of their story on a small sticky note and plot it on the map.

❷ Have students make a drawing to illustrate a main event in their story. Give students an opportunity to tell or write about how they decided what was the main event.

FOLK AND FAIRY TALES FROM AROUND THE WORLD

NAME:_____

DATE:_____

Go to the Web site at the URL below. Click on a country and choose a story to read.

Folk and Fairy Tales from Around the World
URL: http://darsie.ucdavis.edu/tales

1. Complete the following.

Name of my story _____

Country or culture that it comes from _____

Main Characters

_____

_____

_____

_____

_____

_____

_____

_____

_____

2. In the boxes, write the order of things that happened in the story.

What's So Funny?

Overview

Students visit a Web site and read Knock Knock jokes submitted by elementary age children. They choose a joke and explain the word play that makes it funny. Then they write their own joke and explain the word play.

Time Frame

One 45-minute session

Objectives

• Recognize word play.
• Write clear explanations.

Materials

• Computer with Internet access

Procedure

1 Start this activity by telling students the following Knock Knock joke.

Teacher: Knock knock
Students: Who's there?
Teacher: Wayne
Students: Wayne who?
Teacher: Wayne, Wayne go away; come again another day.

2 Ask students to explain what makes the joke funny, or what word is being played on. Explanations might include such comments as: *Wayne* sounds like *rain*; "Rain, rain go away, come again another day" is a line from a well-known nursery rhyme; the name *Wayne* is being used instead of *rain* and the person wants Wayne to leave.

3 Let students tell any Knock Knock jokes that they remember. Have the them explain what makes the jokes funny.

4 Have students go to the URL below to find Kaitlyn's Knock Knock Jokes and Riddles Web site. Explain that students will click on *Knock Knock Jokes* and read them. Then they will write some on their activity sheets and explain what words are being played on and how the word play makes the joke funny.

Knock Knock Jokes and Riddles
URL: http://www.bayne.com/kaitlyn/default.html

5 Provide time for some students to read the jokes they selected and explain the word play that makes them funny.

WHAT'S SO FUNNY?

NAME:_____

DATE:_____

Go to Kaitlyn's Knock Knock Jokes and Riddles Web site at the
URL below.

Knock Knock Jokes and Riddles
URL: http://www.bayne.com/kaitlyn/default.html

Click on *Knock Knock Jokes* and read them.

1. Choose a Knock Knock joke that you read. Write it here. Then
explain what makes it funny.

_____

_____

_____

_____

_____

_____

_____

_____

_____

_____

2. Write another Knock Knock joke. Explain what makes it funny.

_____

_____

_____

_____

_____

_____

_____

_____

_____

_____

TELEPHONE DIALOG

Overview

The Rag Doll, written by Yvonne Augustin, is a delightfully poignant story about a young African American girl who must adjust to her family moving to Chicago. An old rag doll and a story about her great great great grandmother helps Krissie come to terms with leaving her friends and plans behind. After reading the story, students write dialog for a telephone conversation between Krissie and one of her friends that she left behind in Kansas.

Time Frame

Two 45-minute sessions

Objectives

• Write in response to literature.
• Write dialog.

Materials

• Computer with Internet access

Procedure

1 Tell students that you are going to read an online story about a young girl who has something handed down to her that once belonged to her great great great grandmother. Ask students if anyone in their family, or anyone they know, owns something that was handed down from a previous generation.

2 Then go to story at the URL listed below and read the story aloud while the students follow along. Alternatively, you may want to print the story and distribute copies.

The Rag Doll
URL: http://the-office.com/bedtime-story/ragdoll.htm

3 Explain to students they will write dialog for a telephone conversation between Krissie and one of her friends that she had to leave.

4 When students finish writing, pair them to practice reading each other's dialog. Then provide time for students to read in small groups or to share with the whole class.

TELEPHONE DIALOG

NAME:_____

DATE:_____

Write dialog for a telephone conversation between Krissie and one of her friends back in Kansas.

_____

_____

_____

_____

_____

_____

_____

_____

_____

_____

_____

_____

Continue your dialog for a telephone conversation between Krissie and one of her friends back in Kansas.

_____

_____

_____

_____

_____

_____

_____

_____

_____

_____

_____

_____

_____

_____

_____

LOOKING FOR ADJECTIVES

Overview

In this straightforward activity, students read a fun online story and identify the adjectives they find on each page.

Time Frame

One 45-minute session

Objectives

- Use reading skills.
- Identify adjectives.

Materials

- Computer with Internet access

Procedure

1 Introduce this activity by reviewing adjectives. Write the following sentence on the chalkboard.

The little <u>boy</u> was eating a sloppy <u>sucker</u> that he bought from the skinny bald-headed <u>druggist</u> at the tiny <u>market</u>.

2 With students' help, underline each noun in the sentence, as shown. Then ask students to identify the words that tell something about each noun. Be sure students identify the words *little, sloppy, skinny, bald-headed* and *tiny*. Explain that these words that modify nouns are called adjectives.

3 Have students go to the McFeeglebee's Pond online story at the URL below. Explain that they will read the story and then write the adjectives they find on each page.

McFeeglebee's Pond
URL: http://www.magickeys.com/books/mcfee/mpp1.html

Remind students to scroll down each page in order to be able to click on the next page of the story.

Extension

It can be fun for students to make up sentences with a whole bunch of adjectives. Encourage nonsense sentences, as long as the adjectives are used correctly.

LOOKING FOR ADJECTIVES

NAME:_____

DATE:_____

Go to the online story at the URL below.

McFeeglebee's Pond
URL: http://www.magickeys.com/books/mcfee/mpp1.html

Read the story and write at least one of the adjectives you find on each page. Write *none* if there aren't any.

Page 1

_____

_____

_____

Page 2

_____

_____

_____

Page 3

_____

_____

_____

Page 4

_____

_____

_____

Page 5

_____

_____

_____

Page 6

_____

_____

_____

Page 7

_____

_____

_____

Page 8

_____

_____

_____

HOMOPHONE FUN

Overview

Students go to a Web site that has a long list of homophones, each with a simple dictionary definition. They look up a homophone for some given words and then write complete sentences using both words in the same sentence.

Time Frame

One 45-minute session

Objectives

• Identify homophones.
• Write complete sentences.

Materials

• Computer with Internet access

Procedure

1 Write the following pairs of homophones on the chalkboard.

here	hear
heard	herd
sea	see

Explain to students that the pairs of words on the chalkboard are homophones. Homophones are words that are pronounced, or sound, the same but have different meanings and spellings. Have a volunteer read each set of words.

2 Review with the students the meaning of each word and have them use each word in a sentence. Then ask the students to think of a sentence that has both of the homophones *here* and *hear* in it. Then have the students make up sentences using the other two pairs of homophones.

3 Have students go to Alan Cooper's Homonyms Web site at the URL below. Explain that although Alan Cooper calls his list Homonyms, it really is a list of both homophones and homonyms. (Homonyms are words that are both spelled and sound alike but have different meanings. For example, a quail is a bird, but *to quail* means to cower or draw back.) Alan Cooper says on his home page that he knows the difference between homonyms and homophones and that he knows that he has really compiled a list that includes both, yet he still prefers to call his list just homonyms.

Homonyms
URL: http://www.cooper.com/alan/homonym_list.html

Note: The site can be slow to load. You might want to download it ahead of time.

4 Have students look up a homophone for each word on their activity sheet. Then they should write a sentence that uses both words.

HOMOPHONE FUN

NAME:_____

DATE:_____

Go to Alan Cooper's Homonyms Web site at the URL below.

Homonyms
URL: http://www.cooper.com/alan/homonym_list.html

Write a homophone for each word. Then write a sentence that uses both words in the same sentence.

1. real

   Homophone: _____

   Sentence: _____

2. blew

   Homophone: _____

   Sentence: _____

3. wail

   Homophone: _____

   Sentence: _____

···

4. some

   Homophone: _____

   Sentence: _____

5. pour

   Homophone: _____

   Sentence: _____

6. close

   Homophone: _____

   Sentence: _____

7. piece

   Homophone: _____

   Sentence: _____

8. ate

   Homophone: _____

   Sentence: _____

REVISING SNEETCH BALL INSTRUCTIONS

Overview

Among the various links on the Seussville Web site are the instructions for a fun game to play at the beach—Sneetch Ball. Students read the directions and then rewrite them with several changes in mind.

Time Frame

Two or three 45-minute sessions

Objectives

• Write with an awareness of audience.
• Write with the intention of explaining.

Materials

• Computer with Internet access

Procedure

1 Have pairs of students visit the Sneetch Ball Web page at the URL below. Tell students to read the directions several times until they feel certain they could explain how to play the game.

Sneetch Ball
URL: http://www.randomhouse.com/seussville/titles/sneetches/ballgame.html

2 Explain to students they will rewrite the instructions for playing Sneetch Ball with some specific changes in mind. The changes include the following.

- The game will be played by first graders.
- The game will be played indoors.
- The children cannot use scissors, so they must use something else to prepare for the game.
- The game needs a new name.

3 After students have written their revised instructions, put them in groups of 4 or 5 to read each other's work and share ideas.

Extension

Arrange with a first grade teacher to let your students teach the game to his or her students. Have each small group work with a group of younger students. Have them read the instructions to the children and then work with them until they can play the game on their own.

When students return from teaching the game, hold a wrap-up discussion about how hard or easy it was to teach the first graders. Did the children understand their instructions? How would your students write the instructions differently next time? Did anything funny or interesting happen? Finally, let your class have an opportunity to play the game as well!

REVISING SNEETCH BALL INSTRUCTIONS

NAME:_____

DATE:_____

Go to the Sneetch Ball Web page at the URL below.

Sneetch Ball
URL: http://www.randomhouse.com/seussville/titles/sneetches/
ballgame.html

Write new instructions for playing Sneetch Ball. Make the following changes.

1. The game will be played by first graders.

2. The game will be played indoors.

3. The children cannot use scissors, so they must use something else to prepare for the game.

4. The game needs a new name.

New Name of Game: _____

Instructions

_____

_____

_____

_____

_____

_____

_____

_____

_____

_____

_____

_____

_____

_____

UNDERSTANDING THE BRAHMIN'S TALE

Overview

Students read an online story called *The Brahmin's Tale*, an ancient tale from India. Then they answer multiple-choice questions about events that happened in the story and discuss the meaning of the tale.

Time Frame

Two 45-minute sessions

Objectives

- Use reading skills.
- Recall details from reading.
- Interpret meaning from a fable.

Materials

- Computer with Internet access

Procedure

1 Provide a brief introduction to the lesson by telling students they will read a fable from ancient India—*The Brahmin's Tale*. Explain that a Brahmin is a person who is identified as a member of the Brahmin caste (or class) of India. People in this caste believe that its members are, by birth, worthy of the highest respect. Tell students that the name of the Brahmin in their story is Krishnan.

2 Have students go to *The Brahmin's Tale* at the URL below to read the story and find out what happens to Krishnan.

The Brahmin's Tale
URL: http://www.CandlelightStories.com/panchintro.htm

3 When students finish reading the story, have them answer the multiple-choice questions on the activity sheet.

4 Bring the whole class together to review the responses to the multiple-choice questions and discuss the meaning of the tale. To begin the discussion, tell students that it is believed that some ancient tales from this part of the world were originally intended as a way of giving advice to a young prince so that he could become a wise king when he grew up. Ask the students what instruction the tale might offer a young man to make him become a wiser king. Some of the ideas that students might suggest include: being careful who you put in prison, not believing everything people tell you, helping people in need, or the idea that help can come from unexpected sources.

5 You might want to wrap up the lesson by asking students to write in their journals about a time when they believed something they were told, only to find out later that it wasn't true. What were the consequences?

UNDERSTANDING THE BRAHMIN'S TALE

NAME:_____

DATE:_____

Read *The Brahmin's Tale* at the URL below.

The Brahmin's Tale
URL: http://www.CandlelightStories.com/panchintro.htm

Circle the letter of the correct answer.

1. Krishnan left home because

   a. he was getting old.

   b. he couldn't find work.

   c. he didn't like his job

2. Krishnan had

   a. a wife and no children.

   b. two children and no wife.

   c. a wife and children.

3. The jaguar's color is

    a. all black.

    b. black with orange spots.

    c. orange with black spots.

4. The jaguar, monkey, and snake

    a. thanked Krishnan for helping them.

    b. told him not to help the man.

    c. both a and b.

5. A goldsmith

    a. makes jewelry.

    b. builds homes.

    c. sells gold coins.

6. The King thought the Brahmin

    a. stole money.

    b. killed the Prince and stole his jewelry.

    c. killed and ate the jaguar.

Issues of the Day

Overview

This is an activity best suited for older students who are interested in talking about current events or topical issues that affect kids or young teens. Students browse through several online newspapers or magazines to read about current issues and then write an article about something that's important to them.

Time Frame

Two or three 45-minute sessions

Objectives

• Select reading material based on personal interest.
• Write an expository composition.
• Write persuasively.

Materials

• Computer with Internet access

Procedure

1 Invite students to visit several of the Web sites below to find online newspapers or current events magazines. Allow them time to browse and read articles that appeal to them. Although these are educational Web sites, some of the material is targeted for children up to the age of 18. For that reason, you may want to review the articles on these sites ahead of time.

Children's Express
URL: http://www.ce.org/interact/post.htm

Time For Kids
URL: http://pathfinder.com/TFK/index.html

2 After students have had time to read some of the online articles, bring the class together to make a list of the issues they found interesting or controversial. Then encourage students to add to the list any other current topics or issues in which they have an interest. Students might add to the list topics such as drugs in schools, guns in schools, more money for schools, bilingual education, or teen smoking. You might suggest a topic if something interesting or controversial is happening in your school or your community.

3 Organize discussion groups according to interest. Explain to the students that after they have time to share their views and listen to each other, they will write an opinion piece on the topic. Emphasize that using their good listening skills during this discussion time will make them better at writing persuasive articles. If they really hear each other's opposing views it will give them more points to argue when writing their opinion pieces.

4 Have students write an article on the topic of their choice. Pair students to edit each other's work. When the work is polished, you might want to allow students to submit their articles to one of the Web sites and/or share them with the class.

ISSUES OF THE DAY

NAME: _____

DATE: _____

Go to these Web sites to read some articles about current events and issues.

Children's Express
URL: http://www.ce.org/interact/post.htm

Time For Kids
URL: http://pathfinder.com/TFK/index.html

Choose a topic that is of interest to you and write your own article.

Title _____

_____

_____

_____

_____

_____

_____

_____

_____

_____

Continue your article in the space below.

_____

_____

_____

_____

_____

_____

_____

_____

_____

_____

_____

_____

_____

_____

_____

ANSWERS

ANSWER KEY

Activity Sheet 1: Rhyming Fun!

1. tent
2. hat
3. smoke
4. tree

Activity Sheet 2: Beside, Below, Above, and More

Possible answers:

1. Above: butterfly, sun, cloud

   Below: flower or dog, or butterfly below the cloud
2. Either box: doghouse, dog, cat
3. Left: flower

   Middle: cat

   Right: flower

   Left: cat

   Middle: flower

   Right: dog

   Left: flower

   Middle: dog

   Right: flower

Activity Sheet 5: Sounds That Letters Sound Like

1. lion
2. bear
3. quail
4. rhinoceros

Activity Sheet 7: Checking Out an Online Dictionary

1. A vat is a large tub that holds liquid.
2. An arch is a curved opening.
3. Kin are your relatives.
4. An ellipse is a flattened circle.
5. A Venus flytrap is a plant that catches and digests bugs.
6. Meerkats are a type of cat that can stand upright. They are from Africa.
7. A quetzal is a beautiful jungle bird with very long tail feathers.
8. You have to hum into a kazoo to make music.

Activity Sheet 8: Some Synonyms and Antonyms

Possible answers:

1. many

2. twinkle, stars

3. beautiful, lovely

4. dark

5. small, tiny, little, puny

6. happy, smiling, laughing

Activity Sheet 10: Teddy Bear Rhymes

1. around

2. do

3. prayers

4. night

Activity Sheet 11: Looking for Contractions

1. None

2. We'll   we will

   they've   they have

   we'll   we will

3. None

4. There's   There is

5. He'll   He will

6. lady's (circled)

Activity Sheet 12: A Fish Fable

1. Clever Fish

2. Wise Fish, Clever Fish, Stupid Fish

3. Wise Fish, Clever Fish

4. Stupid Fish

Activity Sheet 17: Kid's Poems

Possible answers:

Free Verse Poems	Rhyming Poems
Crocodile	Ants in Ant Town
Rain Forest	Cats
Seagull	November
White Spiders	
Earth is Our Home	
Beautiful Mountain	
Miracle Dove	
Butterfly	
The Sea	
Wonderful	
Gonga	
The Mixed Up Zoo	
In a Garden	

Activity Sheet 19: Kokoto

1. marauding: to roam about and raid in search of plunder
2. selective: highly specific
3. poaching: to trespass, to take by illegal methods
4. captive: taken or held prisoner
5. rebound: to spring back, to return
6. prey: an animal hunted or killed for food by another animal
7. decades: groups of ten years
8. complex: involved, complicated, not simple
9. placid: undisturbed, tranquil, calm, quiet

Activity Sheet 23: Looking for Adjectives

Possible answers:

Page 1: big, red, old, oak, magnificent
Page 2: little, lazy, fast
Page 3: grisly
Page 4: pale
Page 5: none
Page 6: slimy, crooked
Page 7: too many
Page 8: big, red, old, oak, magnificent

Activity Sheet 24: Homophone Fun

1. reel
2. blue
3. whale
4. sum
5. pore
6. clothes
7. peace
8. eight

Activity Sheet 26: Understanding *The Brahmin's Tale*

1. b
2. c
3. c
4. c
5. a
6. b

LIST OF WEB SITES

List of Web Sites

Lesson Plan 1
Sesame Street
URL: http://sesamestreet.com/sesame/activities.

Lesson Plan 2
Animal Gallery
URL: http://www.kids-space.org/gallery/_animals/_animals.html

Lesson Plan 3
Seussville
URL: http://www.randomhouse.com/seussville/titles/days

Lesson Plan 4
Picture of Ernie
URL: http://www.sesamestreet.com/sesame/activities/hl/5/1a.htm

Lesson Plan 5
Animal Alphabet
URL: http://www.mrtc.org/~twright/animals/english/alphquiz.htm

Lesson Plan 6
Ask the Cat
URL: http://www.randomhouse.com/seussville/askthecat

Lesson Plan 7
Little Explorers Picture Dictionary
URL: http://www.LittleExplorers.com/Dictionarytitlepage.html

Lesson Plan 8
Coloring King Friday
URL: http://www.pbs.org/rogers/color3.html

Lesson Plan 9
Eyes on Art
URL: http://www.kn.pacbell.com/wired/art/choose.html

Lesson Plan 10
The Mother Goose
URL: http://pubweb.acns.nwu.edu/~pfa/dreadhouse/nursery/rhymes/teddy.html

Lesson Plan 11
Rhymes and Nonsense
URL: http://www.thekids.com/kids/stories/rhymes

Lesson Plan 12
The Three Fish
URL: http://www.thekids.com/kids/stories/fables/fish/fish.html

Lesson Plan 13
Criss-Cross Setup Form
URL: http://www.puzzlemaker.com/CrissCrossSetupForm.asp

Lesson Plan 14
Children's Stories Web site
URL: http://www.itsnet.com/~outward/childstory.html

Lesson Plan 15
Blue Bear Story
URL: http://www.dreambox.com/storybox/bluebear/bookone/cover.htm

Lesson Plan 16
Poetry For Kids Web site
URL: http://www.poetry4kids.com/poems.html

Lesson Plan 17
Earth to Kids Web site
URL: http://www.edf.org/Earth2Kids

Lesson Plan 18
Little Planet Times Web site
URL: http://littleplanettimes.com

Lesson Plan 19
Kokoto
URL: http://www.edf.org/Earth2Kids/kokoto

Lesson Plan 20
Folk and Fairy Tales from Around the World Web site
URL: http://darsie.ucdavis.edu/tales

Lesson Plan 21
Kaitlyn's Knock Knock Jokes and Riddles Web site
URL: http://www.bayne.com/kaitlyn/default.html

Lesson Plan 22
The Rag Doll story
URL: http://the-office.com/bedtime-story/ragdoll.htm

Lesson Plan 23
McFeeglebee's Pond story
URL: http://www.magickeys.com/books/mcfee/mpp1.html

Lesson Plan 24
Alan Cooper's Homonyms Web site
URL: http://www.cooper.com/alan/homonym_list.html

Lesson Plan 25
Sneetch Ball Instructions
URL: http://www.randomhouse.com/seussville/titles/sneetches/ballgame.html

Lesson Plan 26
The Brahmin's Tale
URL: http://www.CandlelightStories.com/panchintro.htm

Lesson Plan 27
Children's Express
URL: http://www.ce.org/interact/post.htm

Time For Kids
URL: http://pathfinder.com/TFK/index.html